AN ILLUSTRATED CATECHISM

THE APOSTLES' CREED
THE SACRAMENTS
THE TEN COMMANDMENTS
PRAYER

TEXT BY INOS BIFFI
ILLUSTRATED BY FRANCO VIGNAZIA

GRACEWING

LTP
LITURGY TRAINING PUBLICATIONS

International Copyright © 1992, 2005
by Editoriale Jaca Book spa, Milano
All rights reserved.

English translation copyright © 1994 by Wm. B. Eerdmans Publishing Co. Used with permission. First published as four volumes in 1994 by Gracewing, 2 Southern Avenue, Leominster, Herefordshire HR6 OQF, England. English language copyright © 2007. This one-volume edition first published 2007. All rights reserved.

No part of this publication may be reproduced, stored in a retrieval system, or transmitted in any form, or by any means, electronic, mechanical, photocopying, recording or otherwise, without the written permission of the publisher.

Illustrated Catechism © 2007 Archdiocese of Chicago: Liturgy Training Publications, 1800 North Hermitage Avenue, Chicago, IL 60622; 1-800-933-1800, fax 1-800-933-7094, e-mail orders@ltp.org. All rights reserved. See our Web site at www.LTP.org.

UK ISBN 978-0-85244-679-9
USA ISBN 978-1-56854-612-4

Prima edizione italiana, 1992–1993. Seconda edizione italiana, Aprile 2005.

All rights reserved.
Printed in Italy.

Nihil Obstat
Reverend Louis J. Cameli, STD
Censor Deputatus
June 27, 2006

Imprimatur
Reverend John F. Canary, DMin
Vicar General
Archdiocese of Chicago
July 7, 2006

The *Nihil Obstat* and *Imprimatur* are official declarations that a book is free of doctrinal and moral error. No implication is contained therein that those who have granted the *Nihil Obstat* and *Imprimatur* agree with the content, opinions, or statements expressed. Nor do they assume any legal responsibility associated with publication.

Unless otherwise indicated, all scripture quotations are from *The New American Bible*, © 1986 Confraternity of Christian Doctrine, Washington, D.C.

CONTENTS

THE APOSTLES' CREED   7

Introduction   9

Jesus Sends His Disciples to Proclaim the Gospel   10

The Teachers of Faith—the Apostles   12

I believe in God, the Father Almighty,   14

Creator of heaven and earth,   16

and in Jesus Christ, His only Son, our Lord,   19

who was conceived by the Holy Spirit,

     born of the Virgin Mary,   20

suffered under Pontius Pilate, was crucified, died . . .   22

. . . and was buried. He descended into hell.   24

The third day He rose again from the dead.   27

He ascended into heaven,   28

and sits at the right hand of God, the Father Almighty.   30

From thence He shall come to judge

     the living and the dead.   32

I believe in the Holy Spirit,   34

the holy Catholic Church,   37

the communion of Saints,   40

the forgiveness of sins,   42

the resurrection of the body,   44

and life everlasting. Amen.   46

THE SACRAMENTS 48

Introduction 49
The Sacraments: Acts of Jesus 52
Baptism 54
Confirmation 58
The Eucharist 62
Reconciliation 66
Anointing of the Sick 68
Holy Orders 70
Matrimony 72

THE TEN COMMANDMENTS 74

Introduction 76
God's Law for Us 78
I am the Lord your God. 80
1. You shall not have other gods besides me. 80
2. You shall not take the name of the Lord, your God, in vain. 82
3. Remember to keep holy the Sabbath day. 84
4. Honor your father and your mother. 86
5. You shall not kill. 89
6. You shall not commit adultery. 90
7. You shall not steal. 92
8. You shall not bear false witness against your neighbor. 94
9. You shall not covet your neighbor's wife. 96
10. You shall not covet your neighbor's possessions. 98

PRAYER 101

Introduction	103
Humanity in Search of God	104
The Covenant between God and Humanity	106
The Acceptable Gifts of Abel and Noah	108
The Prayers of Abraham and Moses	110
The Prayers of Elijah, Job, Jonah, Hannah, and David	112
Signs, Places, and Times of Prayer	115
Three Wonderful Prayers: "Magnificat," "Benedictus," and "Nunc dimittis"	116
The Prayer of Jesus	118
"Knock and the door will be opened to you"	120
"Lord, teach us to pray": The Lord's Prayer	122
Our Father, who art in heaven, hallowed be thy name; thy kingdom come;	124
thy will be done on earth as it is in heaven.	126
Give us this day our daily bread; and forgive us our trespasses, as we forgive those who trespass against us;	129
and lead us not into temptation, but deliver us from evil. Amen.	130
The Church at Prayer	133
Sunday Prayer and Daily Prayer	134
Communal Prayer and Personal Prayer; Spoken Prayer and Silent Prayer	136
Prayers	138

The Apostles' Creed

Introduction

The purpose of this section is very simple: to teach Christian children the Apostles' Creed. For everyone, regardless of age, the Apostles' Creed is the symbol of faith, its identification card, so to speak. As we become adults and gradually develop a deeper understanding of faith, we are simply expanding our understanding of the precepts of the Apostles' Creed, in its precise and precious formulas, which are ancient yet always new, and which were developed almost immediately and with great care by the Church. The Church repeats them always and never ceases to find new meaning in them.

For children, memorizing the Apostles' Creed represents a significant and beneficial contact with the faith of their parents, of the Christian community in which they live. This section is designed so that parents or other adults can guide children through the explanation of the Apostles' Creed offered here, expanding upon the content with their own comments. They will transmit with confidence and passion the faith that they in turn have received, knowing that they now can draw happily and fully upon the Catechism of the Catholic Church.

The illustrations that accompany the text are direct and simple. This encourages children to visualize what they are reading and hearing. We hope that this synthesis of text and pictures will make the instruction here clear and concrete, and that faith will take root in both the minds and the hearts of the children who study this book, so that they may grow in both knowledge of the faith and good works.

Jesus Sends His Disciples to Proclaim the Gospel

When Jesus rose from the dead, before he ascended into heaven to be near his Father, he sent his disciples — his followers — to proclaim to all people the joyous announcement of salvation, which is the Gospel. After Jesus ascended into heaven, he sent the Holy Spirit to accompany the disciples on this mission. Those people who had faith would be saved.

The Teachers of Faith
— the Apostles

Jesus had many disciples, and from among them he chose the twelve apostles. Peter was the first apostle and the leader of the group. The apostles did not replace Jesus but were his representatives here on earth. (Of course, Jesus is always present in the Church.) In Jesus' name, and with the authority that they received from him, the apostles governed the church. The bishops are the successors of the apostles. They are led by the bishops of Rome, the Pope, who is the successor of Peter. Those who listen to them listen to Jesus Christ.

I believe in God,

the Father Almighty,

Forever and above all, there is God — one God in three Persons: the Father, the Son and the Holy Spirit. Therefore, forever and above all, there is the Trinity. No one has ever seen God, except Jesus, the Son of God. By coming to earth and becoming a man, Jesus revealed God to us. When Jesus was baptized, God clearly indicated his relationship with him. The heavens opened, and the Holy Spirit descended upon Jesus in the form of a dove, and a voice spoke. It was the voice of the Father, who said, "This is my beloved Son" (Matt. 3:17). This is the main precept of the Apostles' Creed.

Creator of heaven and earth,

God is all-powerful. He is the Creator who freely made all things from nothing — visible, like plants and animals, and invisible, like the angels. There was nothing until he created it. And without him, nothing would exist.

God is Love, and he looks after his creatures with love — particularly us, because we are made in his image. God is not the source of evil. Evil came into the world because of the rebellious angels like Satan and because of the disobedience of the first man, Adam. Because of Adam, all of us are born with the sign of that sin: the original sin.

and in Jesus Christ, his only Son, our Lord,

God is the Father, and from eternity, Jesus Christ is his Son, the second Person of the Trinity. Saint John, the evangelist, said of Jesus, "In the beginning was the Word [meaning Jesus, who testified to God's existence], and the Word was with God, and the Word was God. He was in the beginning with God. All things came to be through him, and without him nothing came to be. What came to be through him was life, and this life was the light of the human race" (John 1:1-4). Jesus was the cause, the model and the purpose of creation. And in a special way, man and woman were created in his image. Jesus is the Lord of all, because he loves and offers salvation to everyone, even those who do not yet know him.

who was conceived by the Holy Spirit,

born of the Virgin Mary,

Jesus is the Son of God who became a true man. He was born in Bethlehem to Mary and Joseph. Jesus was miraculously conceived by the Holy Spirit, because God can do all things. Mary, Jesus' mother, carried Jesus in her womb with faith and love, and Saint Joseph, her husband, looked after Jesus with the love of a father.

suffered under Pontius Pilate, was crucified, died …

Jesus spent his life preaching the Gospel, pardoning sinners, casting out demons, healing the sick, revealing the Father's love for everyone, and instructing people to love one another. This was what his Father wanted him to do, but there were people in power who didn't believe in him, so he was condemned to death. He was condemned above all because he proclaimed himself to be the Son of God. By making this declaration and standing by it, Jesus remained faithful to God, and by dying on the cross he offered himself to God as a sign of love, as a sacrifice for our sins. Because of this, our sins are forgiven, and we receive the grace to become children of God. Jesus himself had declared that he had not come into this world to be served, but rather to serve others and to give his life in order to free all people.

    Because of Adam's disobedience, we were lost, but because of Jesus' obedience, we are saved.

... and was buried. He descended into hell.

After Jesus died, his body was removed from the cross and taken to a tomb, which remained sealed for three days. But the soul of Jesus descended into hell, into the realm of the dead. There he freed those who had waited for him as their Redeemer, and he took them to heaven, to be near his Father, in the joy of eternal life. Jesus also proclaimed the Gospel to them and announced the grace of salvation, which had been accomplished by his death on the cross. In this way, the patriarchs — Abraham, Isaac, and Jacob — the prophets, and righteous people who had lived before Jesus' time were able to enter Paradise.

The third day he rose again from the dead.

Jesus conquered death and rose again after three days, leaving his tomb empty (Mark 16:6). In his glorified body, he appeared to selected followers. At first they doubted that the figure before them was their leader, but soon they became joyously convinced that the crucified Christ was indeed alive. The disciples walked with Jesus and talked with him and ate with him, and they bear witness to the fact that Jesus came back from the dead, and wasn't just a phantom or a beautiful dream.

It is extremely important that Jesus did not remain in the tomb. If he had not risen from the dead, our entire faith would be pointless and without foundation. But by conquering the grave, he conquered sin and saved us.

He ascended into heaven,

Before he returned to heaven, the risen Jesus remained close to his disciples for forty days. He helped them to understand the Sacred Scriptures that had predicted his passion and resurrection from the grave. He explained to them God's plan for the conversion and salvation of humanity. And

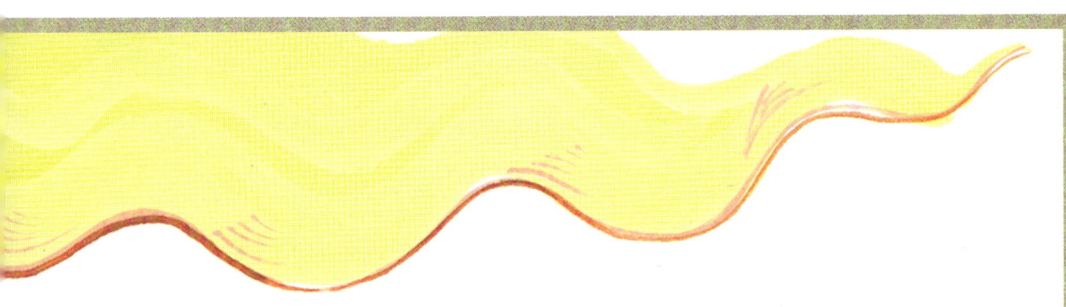

by offering the disciples proof that he was truly alive, he reinforced their certainty about his resurrection, so that they could testify to his resurrection without the slightest shadow of doubt.

Finally, Jesus entrusted the disciples with this mission: "Go, therefore, and make disciples of all nations, baptizing them in the name of the Father, and of the Son, and of the holy Spirit, teaching them to observe all that I have commanded you" (Matt. 28:19-20). And after he told them that he would be with them always, he ascended into heaven.

and sits at the right hand of God, the Father Almighty.

When Jesus ascended into heaven, he was welcomed with great rejoicing by his Father. He had sent Jesus to earth as a gift to us, to bring us salvation. Now, after enduring the humiliation of the cross and triumphing over the grave, Jesus entered the same glory as God the Father, who rewarded him and honored him for his obedience. In the glorified Jesus, all of humanity is exalted. He represents the goal and the heavenly destiny of all humanity, whom he calls to himself. His ascension did not mean that he had abandoned us or distanced himself from us. As he promised, "I am with you always, until the end of the age" (Matt. 28:20).

From thence he shall come to judge the living and the dead.

At the end of time, Jesus will come to judge all humankind. Only God knows the time of this second coming. But even though we do not see Jesus now as he will appear then, in his glorious manifestation, he is always present here on earth, and he can appear at any moment. And we know that we will see him on the day that we die. What is important right now is to live like his faithful and watchful disciples, keeping hope alive while we wait for him. All authority and power in heaven and on earth belong to him. He will closely judge the life and the actions of every human being. Through his judgment, which is both merciful and final, each person will receive eternal rewards in heaven or eternal suffering in hell.

I believe in
the Holy Spirit,

After he had ascended into heaven, the Lord Jesus, together with his Father, sent the Holy Spirit, the third person of the Trinity, to his followers on the feast of Pentecost. The Holy Spirit was already at work in the world: he had participated in the creation, and had appeared in the form of a dove at Jesus' baptism, and was inspiring the writing of the Holy Scriptures. It is the Holy Spirit who now makes Jesus present in the world and teaches us to know and love him.

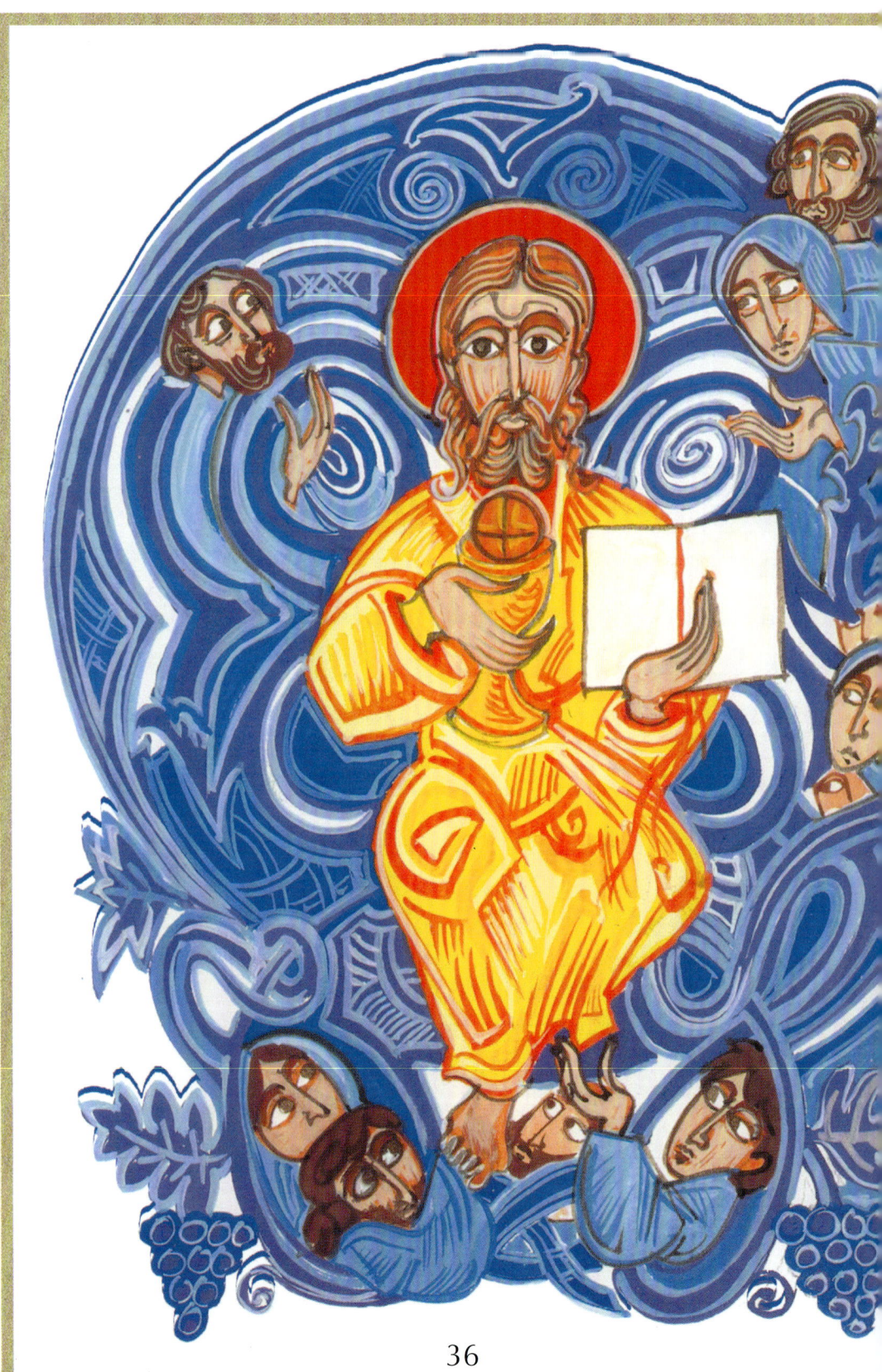

the holy Catholic Church,

The Church came into being on Pentecost, when the Father, through his glorified Son, Jesus, sent the Holy Spirit upon Jesus' followers. The Church is formed by those who convert, who believe in the Gospel, who are baptized, who are strengthened by the Lord through the Eucharist, and who live like children of God. All of this is possible through the grace of the Holy Spirit, who makes us recognize Jesus and inspires faith in him. It is the Holy Spirit who regenerates those who are baptized; it is the Holy Spirit who transforms bread and wine into the

Body and Blood of Christ during the Eucharist; it is the Holy Spirit who lives in the hearts of the faithful and makes their actions conform to those of Jesus.

The Church is the people of God; it is the body of Christ. The Church is one, even though there are many Christian communities around the world, because it is united by Jesus through the Holy Spirit. The Church is holy because it was formed by the followers of God, who were sanctified by the Holy Spirit. The Church is catholic because all people are called to be part of it. The Church is apostolic because it was founded upon the testimonies of the apostles, who were succeeded by the bishops, led by the head bishop, the Pope.

The Church is the effective and necessary sign for salvation. Those who sincerely seek God already begin to belong to the Church in their hearts. All of the holiness and beauty of the Church will be perfected in heaven.

the communion of saints,

The Church is a community of saints. Those who are already in heaven intercede on our behalf, together with Mary, the mother of Jesus and the mother of us all. Together with the saints in heaven, there are the faithful, the pilgrims on earth, who share the same faith, the same body of Christ, the same Spirit. Even the dead who are being purified in Purgatory are members of this one family of God.

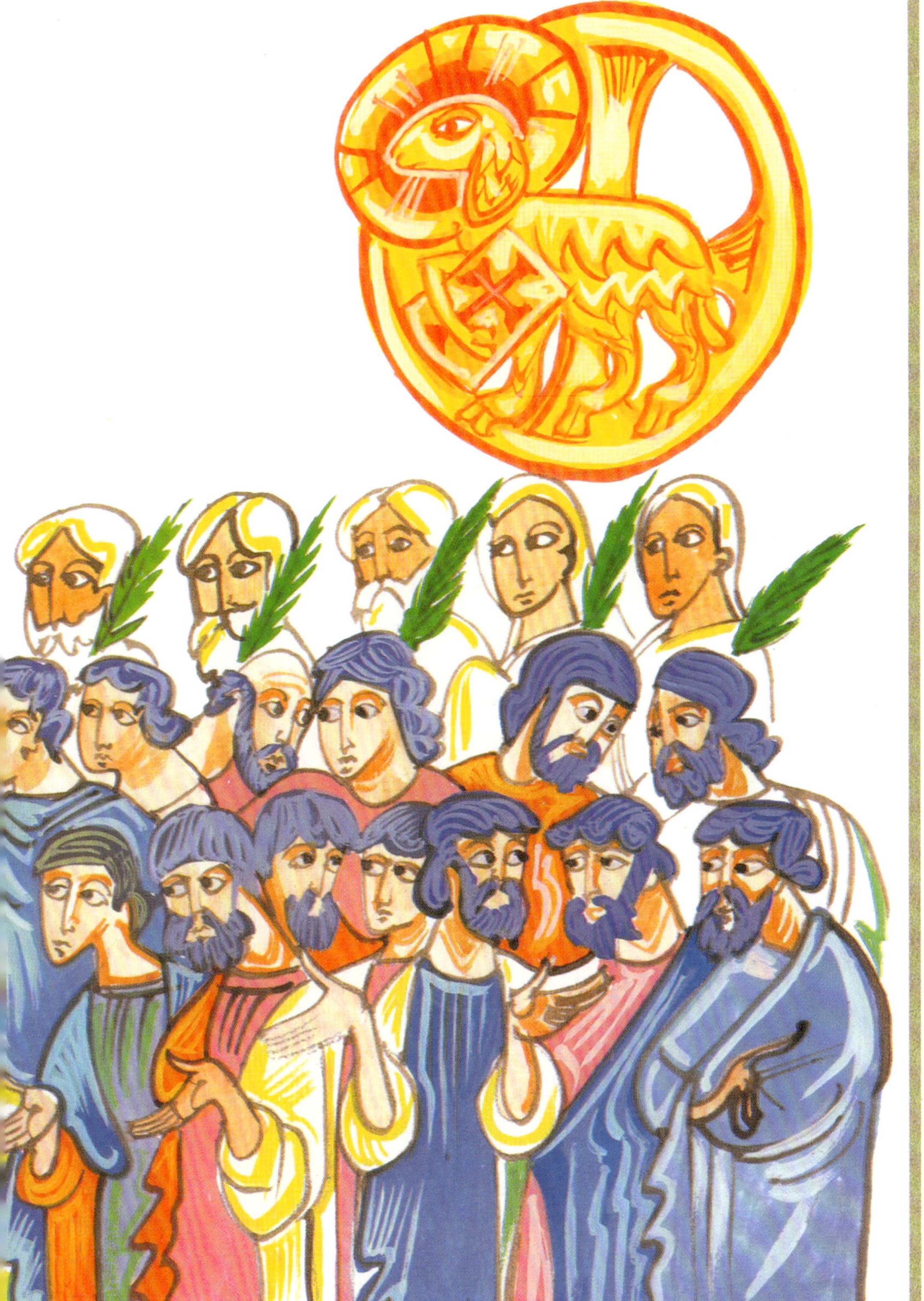

the forgiveness

When we are born, we do not yet possess the dignity and sanctity of children of God. Instead, our souls all mysteriously bear the sign of the sin of Adam, which is sadly renewed in each sin that we commit. But the risen Jesus gave us the Holy Spirit for the forgiveness of sins, which he earned for us through his death on the cross. God offers everyone the grace of forgiveness. The Church is

# of sins,

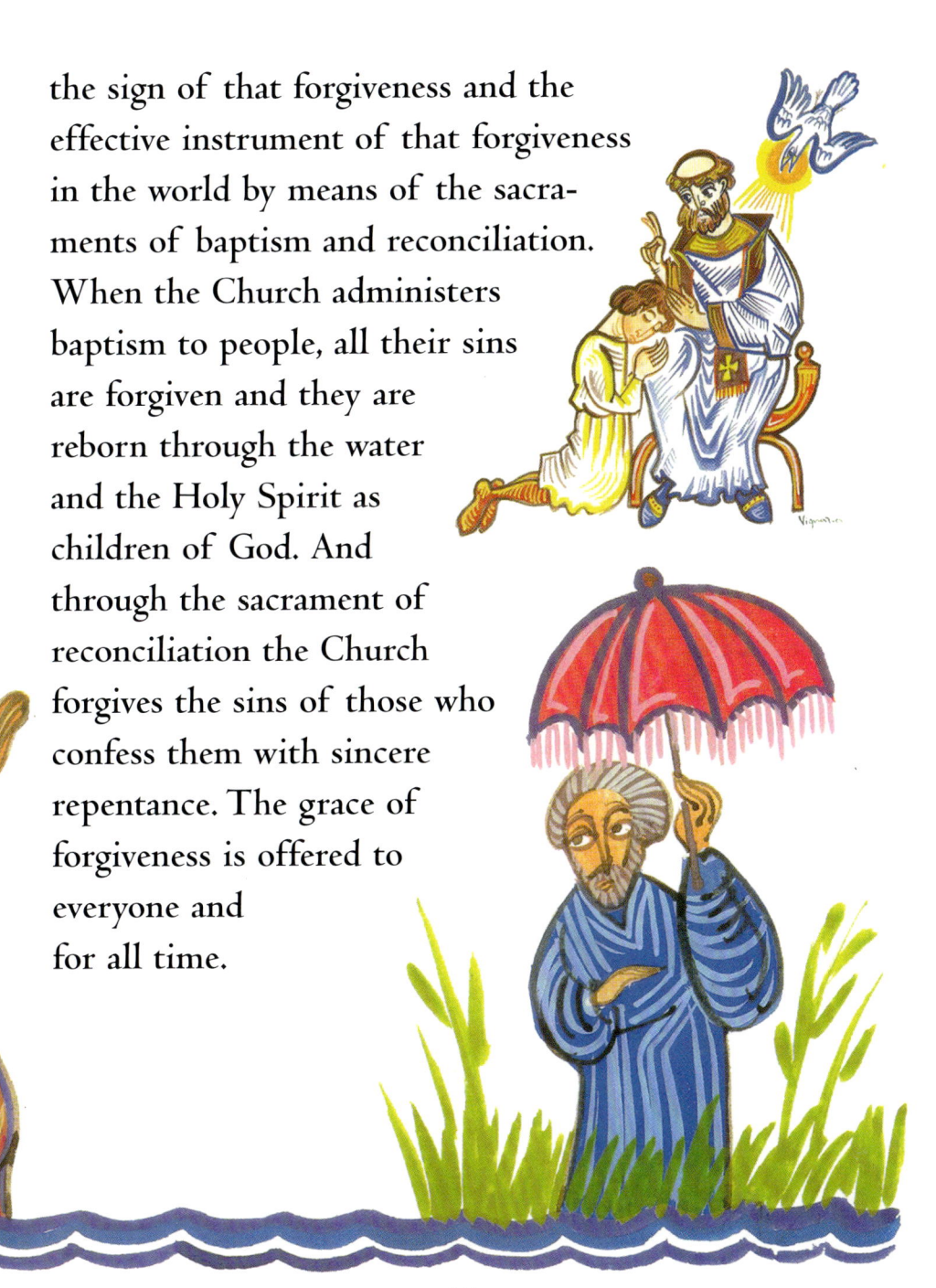

the sign of that forgiveness and the effective instrument of that forgiveness in the world by means of the sacraments of baptism and reconciliation. When the Church administers baptism to people, all their sins are forgiven and they are reborn through the water and the Holy Spirit as children of God. And through the sacrament of reconciliation the Church forgives the sins of those who confess them with sincere repentance. The grace of forgiveness is offered to everyone and for all time.

the resurrection of

Death came into the world as a punishment for sin. By rising again from the dead, Jesus overcame sin and death for all humankind. All those who live and die in communion with Jesus, who is "the resurrection and the life" (John 11:25), carry within them the seed of resurrection. Because of this, the Holy Spirit can raise them up in the image of the Lord, who was the first to have risen from the dead. Their bodies will also be saved — they will be whole people, united body and soul, in their glory. However, those who die in mortal sin shall be raised from the dead not to enjoy eternal life but to suffer damnation.

the body,

and life everlasting. Amen.

When those who live their lives as children of God die and face the final judgment, they will enter into eternal life, and, together with Jesus and the saints, they will know the unimaginable joy of seeing the Father. But those who have obstinately refused the salvation that God offers to everyone will be condemned to eternal suffering. Purgatory is the place where believers can undergo a final purification before seeing God.

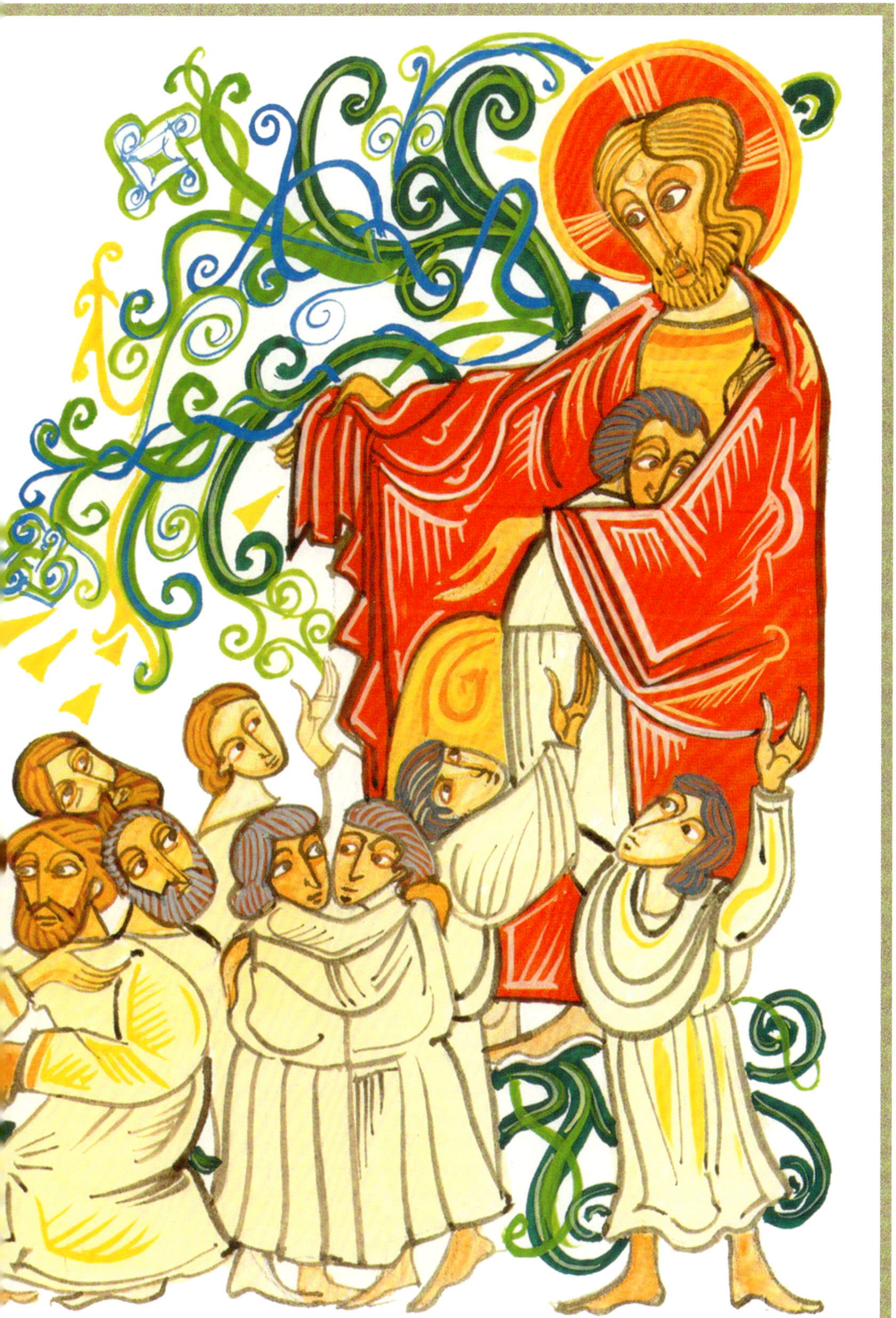

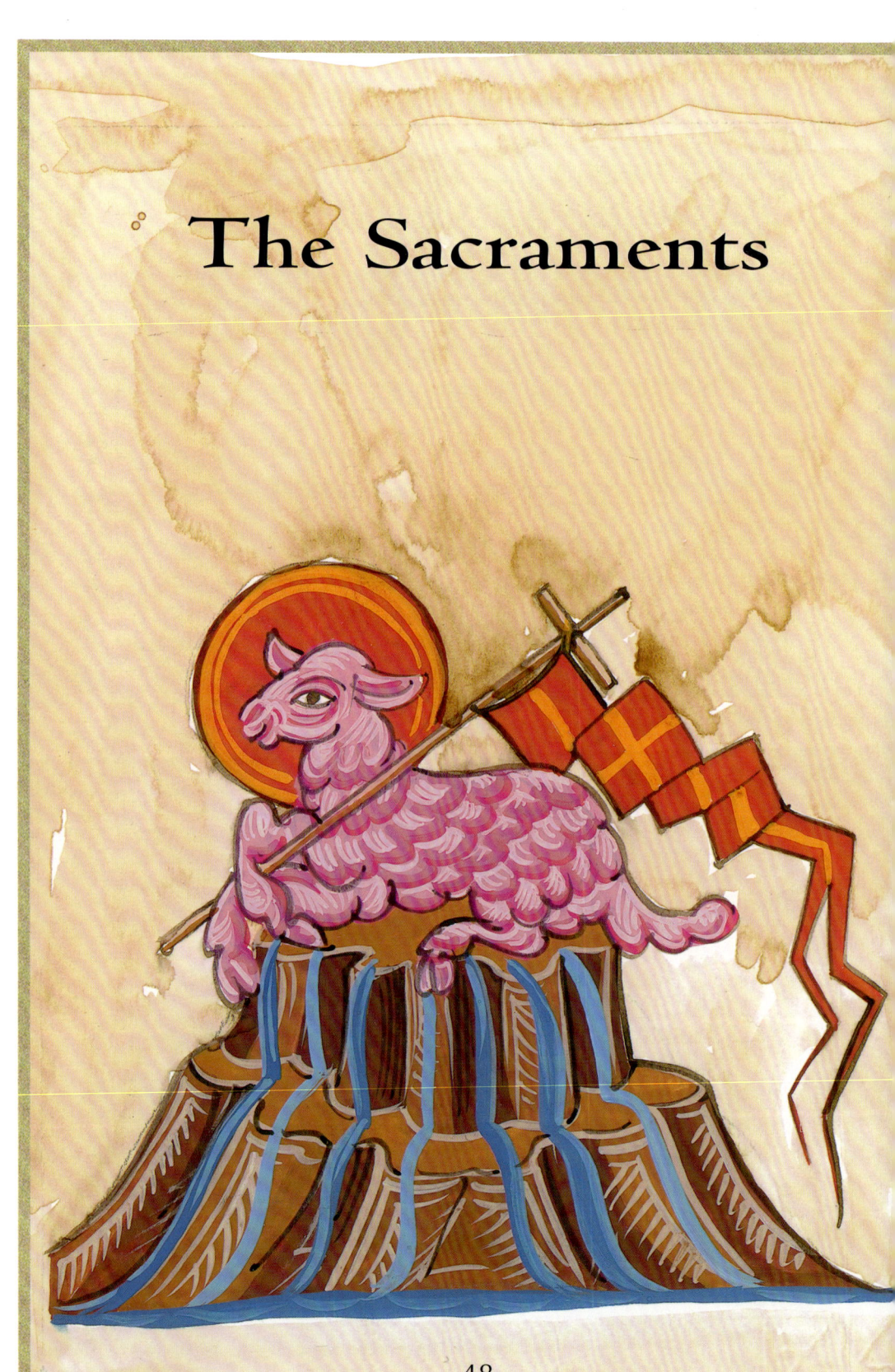

The Sacraments

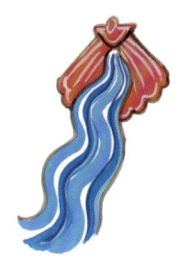

Introduction

This section about the Sacraments is very closely related to the other section about the Apostles' Creed. The Sacraments, as a matter of fact, are rituals that make present in certain ways that which we profess in the Creed. In this part the commentary on the Sacraments is supplemented with clear, simple pictures. Although this combination of explanation and illustration may allow children to grasp some of the concepts on their own, it is essential that they study this section with the guidance of an adult — ideally a parent or a catechist.

It is also essential that children see these Sacraments celebrated in the Church. This will vividly impress these rites on their minds and hearts. With such experiences, augmented by the kind of instruction this book offers, they will be able to begin to understand, appreciate, and desire to participate in these sacred rites, which are the signs, both simple and wonderful, of the Lord's presence in his Church.

50

51

The Sacraments: Acts of Jesus

The Sacraments are visible acts performed by the Church, such as an immersion in water, an anointing with oil, and the celebration of a meal of bread and wine.

But the Sacraments are not only outward actions performed by human beings. They are the actions of Jesus, who instituted them and who makes them have an effect when we perform them. He, together with the Holy Spirit, is truly — even though invisibly — present when the Sacraments are celebrated, just as he is present every time the Church gathers to pray.

On the cross, Jesus gave himself for the salvation of the human race. Through the Sacraments he perpetuates his gift of himself, and our encounter with him is made possible. In the Sacraments, we take part in the passion of Christ, in order to share in his resurrection.

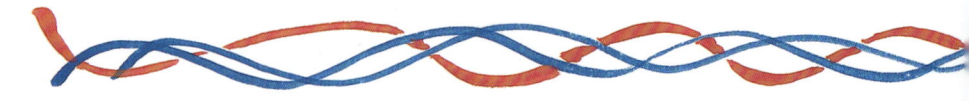

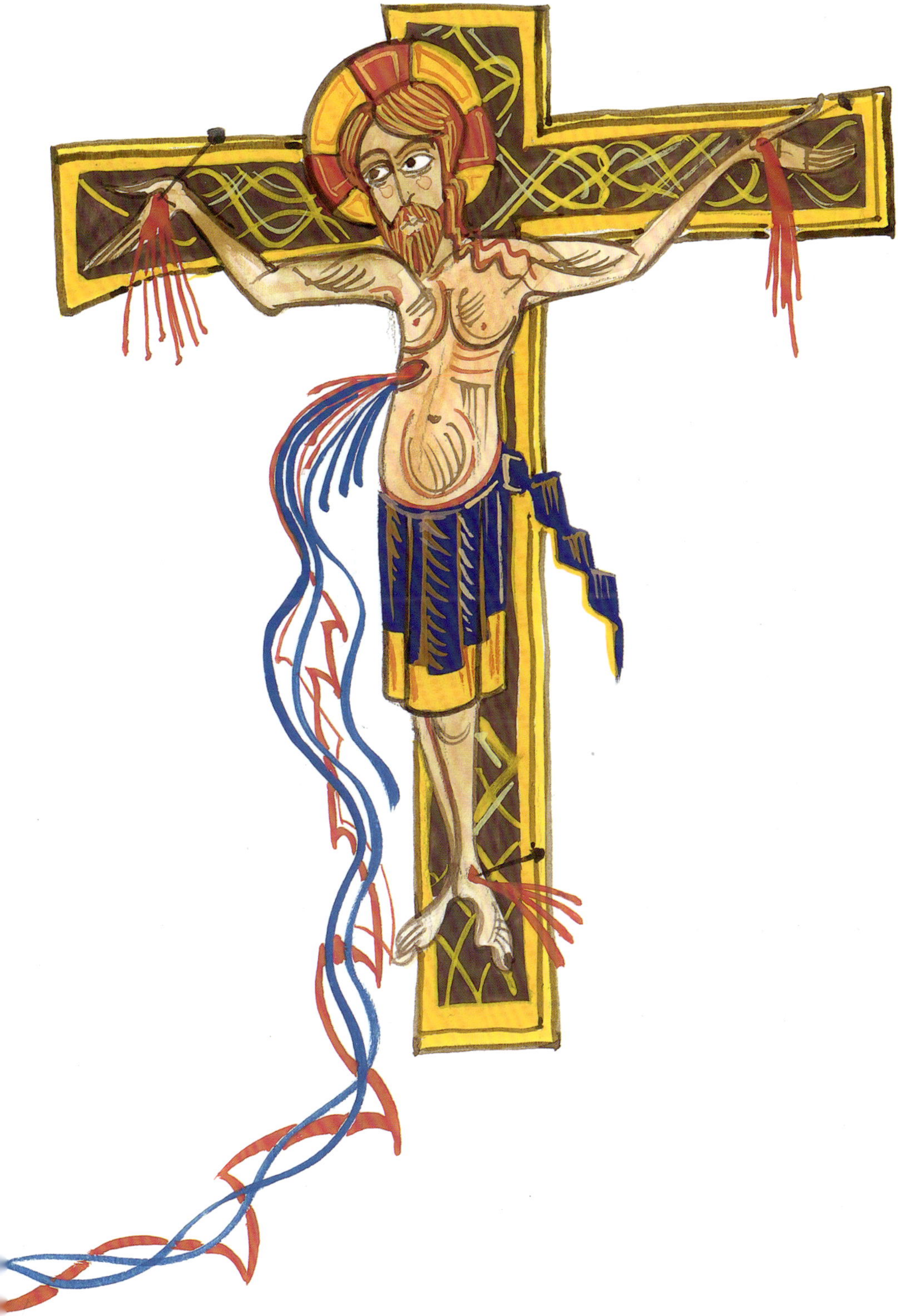

Baptism

It is necessary for us as sinners to be born again "of water and [the] Spirit," Jesus said (John 3:5). For this he has established the sacrament of baptism. The one who administers this sacrament immerses the person being baptized in the baptismal font or pours water on the person's head. During this act, the one performing it says, "I baptize you in the name of the Father, the Son, and the Holy Spirit."

In order to be baptized, it is necessary to believe in the Gospel. As a baby, you were baptized in the baptismal font on the strength of your parents' faith. As you grow up, their faith will become your own personal faith, and you will profess it as your own.

When we are baptized, we become children of God and a new creation, and we begin to be part of

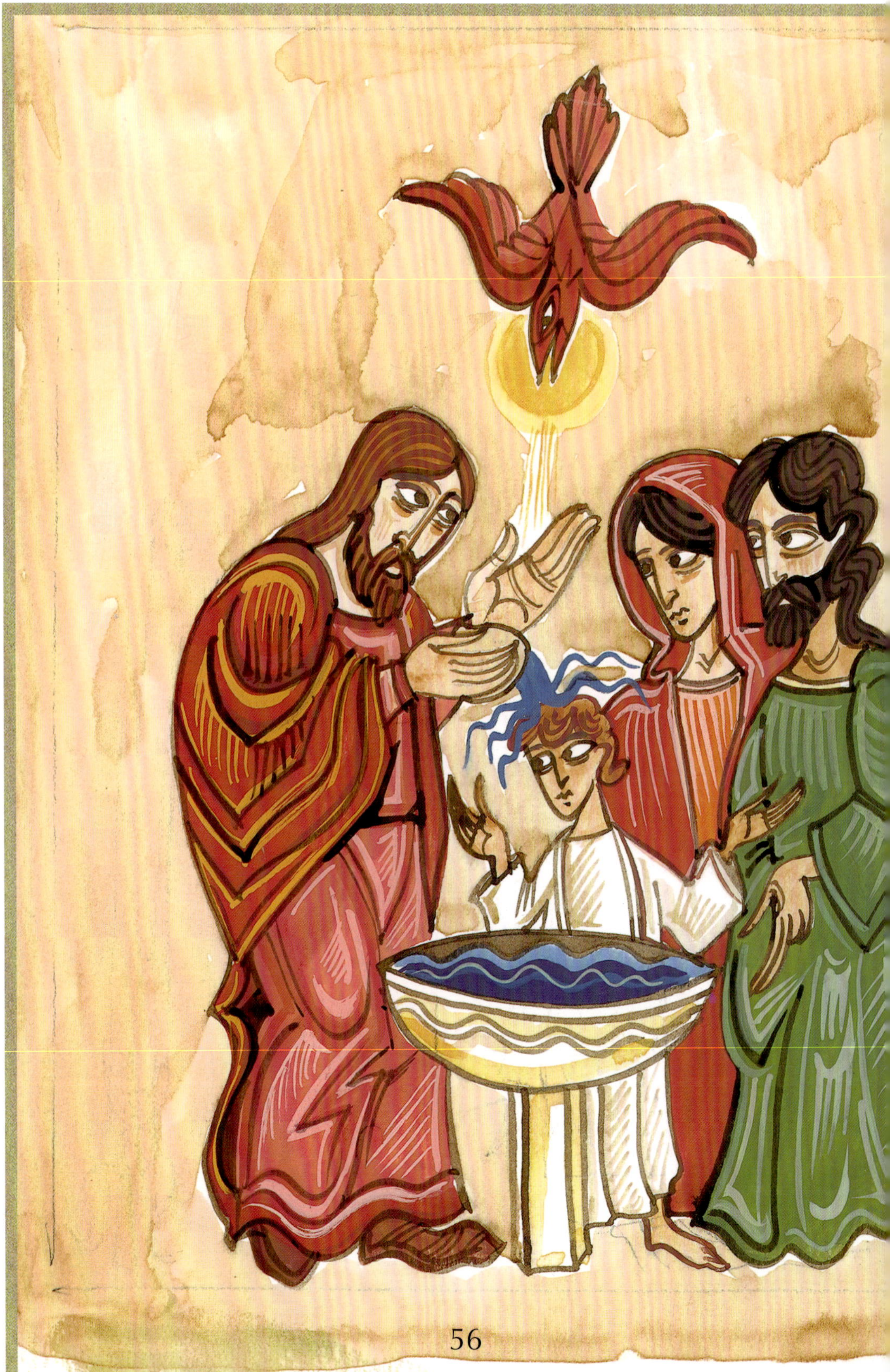

a new family, the Church. The stain of original sin from Adam is blotted out; every one of our own personal sins is pardoned; and it is possible for us to enter into the kingdom of heaven. Baptism imprints a permanent sign on our souls showing that we belong to Jesus Christ; this is called an indelible character.

Confirmation

Baptism is perfected by the sacrament of confirmation. This sacrament is ordinarily administered by a bishop. He anoints the foreheads of those being confirmed with chrism, which is oil mixed with a fragrance to make a balm. During the anointing, he says, "Be sealed with the gift of the Holy Spirit." He then offers them the same blessing that the risen Lord gave his disciples: "Peace be with you".

Like baptism, confirmation imprints on our souls a permanent sign of belonging to Jesus Christ, since in this sacrament the fullness of the Holy Spirit is poured out on us.

With the grace of the Spirit — which descended upon the apostles on the day of Pentecost, and which we have already received in baptism — we become mature Christians. Our likeness to Christ grows, and we become more intimately a part of his Church.

Confirmation renews and strengthens our commitment to be courageous witnesses of the Gospel in the world, both through our words and through our actions.

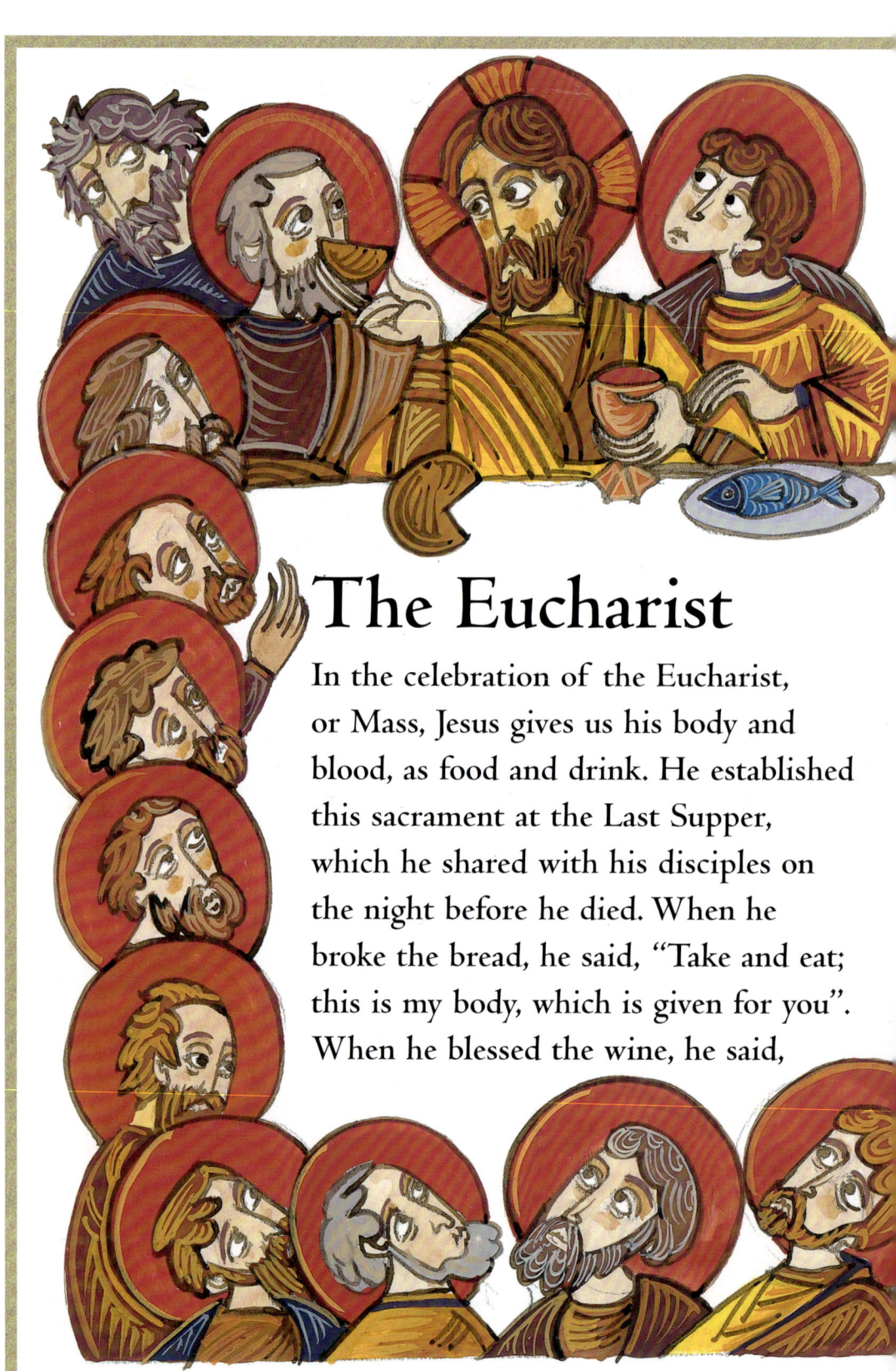

The Eucharist

In the celebration of the Eucharist, or Mass, Jesus gives us his body and blood, as food and drink. He established this sacrament at the Last Supper, which he shared with his disciples on the night before he died. When he broke the bread, he said, "Take and eat; this is my body, which is given for you". When he blessed the wine, he said,

"Take and drink: this is the chalice of my blood poured out for you and for all so that sins may be forgiven. Do this in memory of me." When we celebrate the Eucharist, we perform an act of obedience and faithfulness to this command of our Lord.

At Mass, through prayer and the working of the Holy Spirit, the bread and the wine are changed, or "transubstantiated", into the body and blood of Jesus. In this way, we are united to the Paschal sacrifice offered by Christ on the cross to his Father for our salvation — so that we too receive the strength to love all others like brothers and sisters.

The celebration of the Eucharist gathers the Faithful together, especially on Sunday, the day on which we commemorate the resurrection of the Lord. The priest presides at the sacrament, since he has received the power to do so from Jesus himself. The congregation of the Faithful are not simply spectators; they all participate actively and consciously. The Mass, like all liturgy of the Church, involves the whole people of God: in this rite all believers are bound together. But not everyone can receive Holy Communion. Only those who live in friendship with God — and are not prevented by serious sin — can approach the table of the Body of Christ, in anticipation of the heavenly banquet.

Even after the celebration of Mass, Jesus remains present in the Eucharist. In this way, he can come in communion to the sick and the dying. He can also meet his disciples during solemn Adoration, or be present with them in their silent personal prayer in the Church.

Reconciliation

SYCOMORVS

When he appeared to the disciples on Easter evening, Jesus gave to them and their successors the Holy Spirit for the forgiveness of sins. He said, "If you forgive the sins of any, they are forgiven" (John 20:23, RSV). During his life Jesus himself had forgiven many sins, such as those of the paralyzed man, and those of Zacchaeus, whom he made come down from the tree.

To obtain forgiveness, we must be truly sorry for our sins, confessing them with honesty to the priest, who absolves them in the name of Christ. And we must also make reparation for our sins, especially through acts of charity and the resolution not to commit them again. The forgiveness of sins is God's greatest cause for rejoicing.

Anointing of the Sick

Jesus, who during his life comforted and healed many who were sick, has established a special sacrament for those who are seriously ill because of disease or aging. The priest administers this sacrament. He anoints the body of the sick person with sacred oil while saying this prayer: "Through this holy anointing, may the Lord in his love and mercy help you with the grace of the Holy Spirit. Amen.

May the Lord, who frees you from sin, save you and raise you up. Amen".

This sacrament, when received with faith, gives the sick person the comfort of the Lord risen from death. It gives him serenity and trust so that he doesn't allow himself to be pulled down by his suffering. Instead, he is able to unite his suffering from illness with Jesus' passion and offer it for the good of the whole Church. Through this holy anointing, God will grant the sick person the forgiveness of sins and will prepare him for the passage to eternal life; God is also able to restore the grace of health.

Holy Orders

The sacrament of Holy Orders is conferred on men through the bishop's laying on of hands and pronouncing of the consecratory prayer. Through this sacrament some of the Faithful receive the commission to preside over the Christian community, to preach the Gospel, and to celebrate Mass in the name of and with the power of Jesus. The sacrament of Holy Orders, which (like baptism and confirmation) imprints a permanent mark on the soul, is divided into three degrees. The bishop receives this sacrament in its fullness, and becomes, together with all the other bishops, one of the successors of the apostles. The second degree is received by presbyters, or priests, who are the bishop's closest collaborators. The third degree is received by deacons, who, not being priests and not celebrating Mass, dedicate themselves to serving the Church in various ways: they proclaim and explain the Word of God, they perform certain parts of liturgical rites, and they coordinate many different charitable initiatives.

Those who receive the sacrament of Holy Orders do not replace Jesus Christ but represent him. He acts through them, but always remains the only High Priest.

Matrimony

God himself, who in the beginning created man and woman, has established marriage, through which a couple, united by a mutual, indissoluble, and fruitful love, form a family. The marriage of two disciples of the Lord is a sacrament. The love between two married Christians is a sign of Jesus' love for his Church, and makes that love present. The couple receive from the Lord the grace and the responsibility to love each other always, to be faithful to each other, to never break the bond of their love, and to give life to children and to educate them.

During the celebration of the marriage, the man and the woman make a mutual commitment to each other: "I take you to be my wife" and "I take you to be my husband". Each of them also makes this vow: "I promise to be true to you in good times and in bad, in sickness and in health. I will love you and honor you all the days of my life".

Jesus prohibits divorce. He says, "That which God has united, man must not divide". Only where there is a mutual, sincere and abiding love can human life grow and mature.

The Ten Commandments

I am the Lord your God.

1. You shall not have other gods besides me.

2. You shall not take the name of the Lord, your God, in vain.

3. Remember to keep holy the Sabbath day.

4. Honor your father and your mother.

5. You shall not kill.

6. You shall not commit adultery.

7. You shall not steal.

8. You shall not bear false witness against your neighbor.

9. You shall not covet your neighbor's wife.

10. You shall not covet your neighbor's possessions.

Exodus 20:1-17
Deuteronomy 5:6-21

Introduction

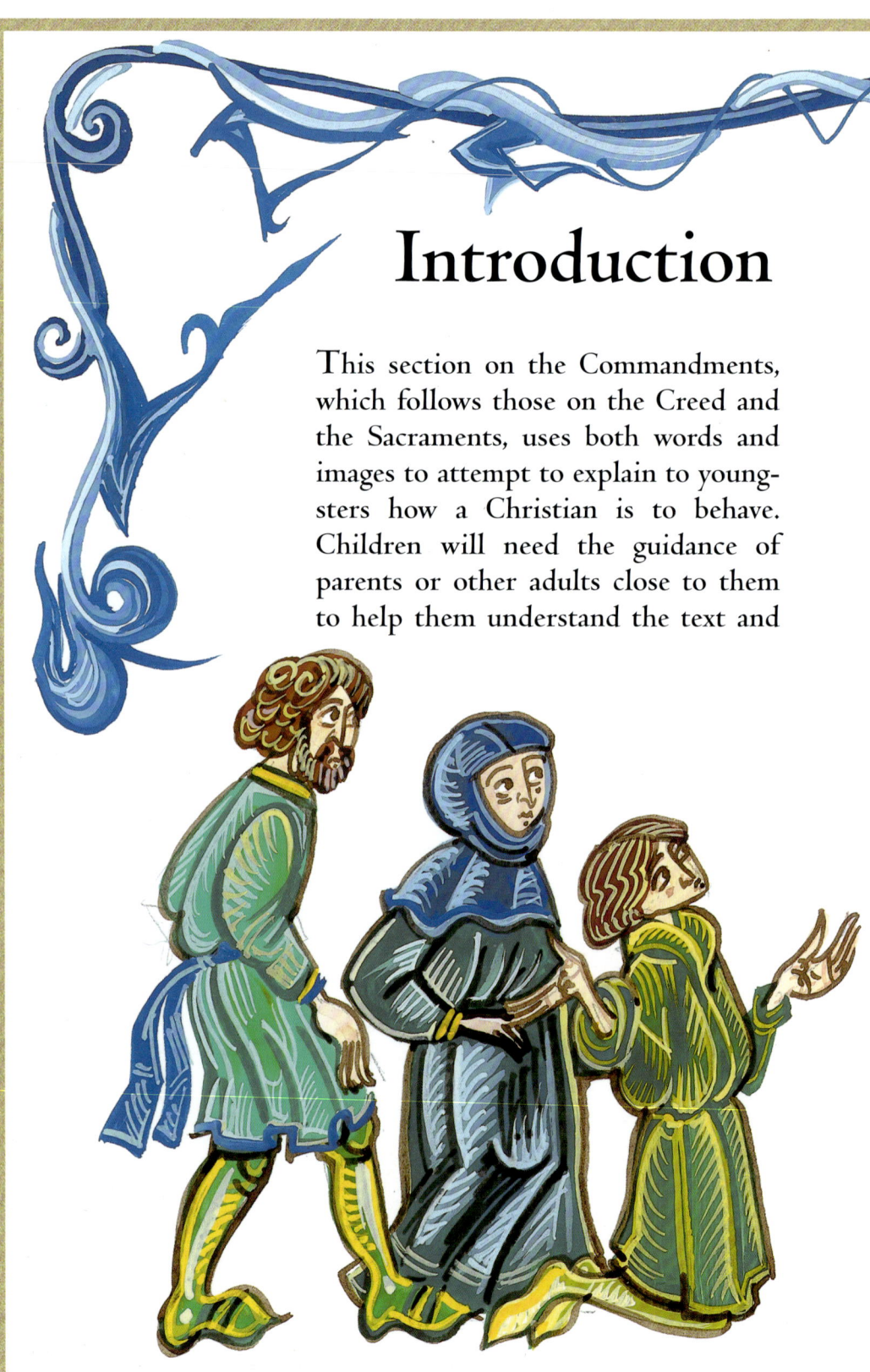

This section on the Commandments, which follows those on the Creed and the Sacraments, uses both words and images to attempt to explain to youngsters how a Christian is to behave. Children will need the guidance of parents or other adults close to them to help them understand the text and illustrations, and, most important, to offer them conviction, instruction, and inspiration by example.

Indeed, the parents will be the first teachers of the Commandments. They will foster in their children the desire for the Law of the Lord. Together they will enroll in the school of Jesus, the only true teacher and model, who said of himself, "I am the light of the world. Whoever follows me will not walk in darkness, but will have the light of life" (John 8:12).

God's Law for Us

When God created Adam and Eve, he gave them a conscience so that they could tell right from wrong, and he gave them the gift of freedom so that they could love and choose goodness, although they could also choose evil. In fact, in the beginning, Adam and Eve disobeyed God and by doing that chose evil, which clouded their hearts. By freely and consciously choosing evil, they sinned against God. But God has not abandoned humanity because of this sin, which is what we call original sin. Indeed, as a sign of his continuing covenant with us, he gave Moses two tablets of stone with the Ten Commandments carved on them. Jesus renewed this ancient Law in a profound way by coming down to earth and dying on the cross. He proclaimed and imprinted on the hearts of his disciples the new Law of the Gospel, which says that we are to love God and love our neighbor.

I am the Lord your God.

I. You shall not have other gods besides me.

There is only one Lord, in three persons: the Father, the Son, and the Holy Spirit. He created us and saved us; he sees the intimate parts of our souls; he follows us constantly with love; he waits for us to come to him so that he can give us eternal joy. Whoever pretends to be God is only a false idol who deceives us and enslaves us.

We respond to the love of God by loving him and praying to him with all our hearts. Prayer is made up of three things: adoration, in which we recognize and praise the Lord as the only God; thanksgiving, through which we acknowledge his gifts to us; and respectful humility, in which we ask for God's help in faith.

There are two kinds of prayer: those we say privately, in our personal devotions at home; and those we say in Church, together with the other disciples of Jesus. This second kind of prayer is called liturgical prayer: it is the source of and model for all our prayers. The Lord Jesus is always present in prayer.

2. You shall not take the name of the Lord, your God, in vain.

God himself revealed his name to Moses, the leader of the Hebrew people. In this way he showed his love for all humanity and his continuous presence with them.

The name of God is a sacred name: it is not to be said in vain, thoughtlessly and without respect, as if it were just any name. One must not swear to something by calling God as a witness unless it concerns a very important matter. Whoever insults God or curses him commits the sin of blasphemy.

We are to use the name of God reverently during prayer and worship. When we call upon God, we are to offer him our praise and express our gratitude and our love, still remembering the warning of Jesus: "Not everyone who says to me, 'Lord, Lord,' will enter the kingdom of heaven, but only the one who does the will of my Father in heaven" (Matt. 7:21).

3. Remember to keep holy the Sabbath day.

Since the time of the apostles, the holy day for Christians is Sunday, which we call the "Day of the Lord". Because Jesus was resurrected on Sunday, the Church chose this day among all other days of the week and made it special. On this day we are to celebrate Holy Mass, engage in charitable acts, restore our spirits, and rest our bodies.

Whoever is without a serious reason for not participating in the Sunday Mass, and who spends this day like any other, seeks amusement immoderately, and shows no interest in the welfare of others has not sanctified this holy day.

4. Honor your father and your mother.

According to the divine design, children are born into a family, from the love between mother and father. In giving life to their children, parents reveal and imitate the goodness and the creative power of God; the children carry within themselves the image of Jesus, the Son of God; and the love that binds the whole family together reflects the love of the Holy Spirit himself, which unites the Father and Jesus.

Mothers and fathers are called to educate their children with sweetness and firmness, especially by setting a good example. They help their children to grow in freedom, to discover their vocation, and to become responsible adults active within the Church and society.

Children express their thanks by obeying their parents and showing them respectful love and care. In particular, they do not neglect their parents when they are old, but remain close to them and assist them lovingly.

88

5. You shall not kill.

God has created us in his image and likeness, and for this reason the life of every person is sacred. Life deserves love and care from the moment it first flickers in a mother's womb until it is extinguished by death. Whoever kills another person imitates the sin of Cain, who killed his brother Abel. But whoever loves others imitates Jesus, who gave his life for us. We must do more than obey the command not to kill, however, we must protect human life and avoid any exploitation, manipulation, or domination of it.

The legitimate defense of human life, both our own and others', is right and proper. What is wrong is suppressing innocent lives, being vengeful, and being aggressive. It is also wrong to take one's own life, because life is a gift of God.

6. You shall not commit adultery.

God made man and woman with an attraction for each other, so that they may join together in marriage, love each other, and give life to children through the intimate sharing of their hearts and their bodies. This commandment condemns unfaithfulness between husband and wife and forbids every impure thought, desire, and act. The bond of marriage requires that husband and wife honor their commitment to each other by sharing their bodies only with each other. Indeed, each of us is to respect and honor our body as a gift from God and a sign of love. The body of a Christian is sanctified by the Holy Spirit's dwelling within it, as within a temple.

7. You shall not steal.

Stealing means taking away what belongs to another person. God forbids stealing because he is concerned that the goods of the earth be divided justly, so that all people can have what they need to live with dignity, as men and women.

Those who do not adequately pay the people who work for them and those who keep so much wealth that they force others to endure in poverty, hunger, unemployment, underdevelopment, and inhuman conditions disobey this commandment. In the same way, this commandment is broken by those who get rich at the expense of the community and do not contribute to the good of that community, and by those who earn their living dishonestly and take advantage of others.

8. You shall not bear false witness against your neighbor.

Jesus said of himself, "I am the truth" (John 14:6), and he called the devil "a liar and the father of lies" (John 8:44).

If we want to imitate Jesus, we must reject every form of falsehood. We must not deceive, cheat, or lie. We must love truth, and we must search for it with commitment and speak it with courage, even if it means making a sacrifice. We must strive to be pure, loyal, sincere, and discreet. We must not believe everything we hear, and we must keep the promises we make and keep the confidences that others entrust to us. And we must always remember the admonition of Jesus: "Let your 'Yes' mean 'Yes' and your 'No' mean 'No', that you may not incur condemnation" (James 5:12).

9. You shall

We have already seen that in the beginning God created man and woman so that they would be united by a faithful and enduring love and, through marriage, would form a family. They would join together in a sacred union to pass on life to their children, whom they would love and educate in the ways of God.

not covet your neighbor's wife.

Marital love is especially sacred between two Christians, because their union was consecrated by Jesus with a sacrament. For this reason, God prohibits desiring another person's spouse, thinking of that man or woman as an object to be possessed. He severely condemns whoever tries to break the union between husband and wife. And Jesus has added, "Everyone who looks at a woman with lust has already committed adultery with her in his heart" (Matt. 5:28).

10. You shall not covet your neighbor's possessions.

In the last commandment, God warns us not to envy the possessions of others, thus not fostering in our hearts the love of riches. Those people who are anxious to acquire earthly goods become slaves to material things; they become selfish and insensitive to the needs of others; they commit unjust acts simply to possess certain objects.

Jesus did not choose a life of luxury for himself; he chose a life of poverty and simplicity. And he proclaimed that the poor are blessed because they are saved from the dangers of wealth. Let us listen to his words: "Do not store up for yourselves treasures on earth … But store up treasures in heaven … What profit would there be for one to gain the whole world and forfeit his life?" (Matt. 6:19-20; Matt. 16:26).

100

Prayer

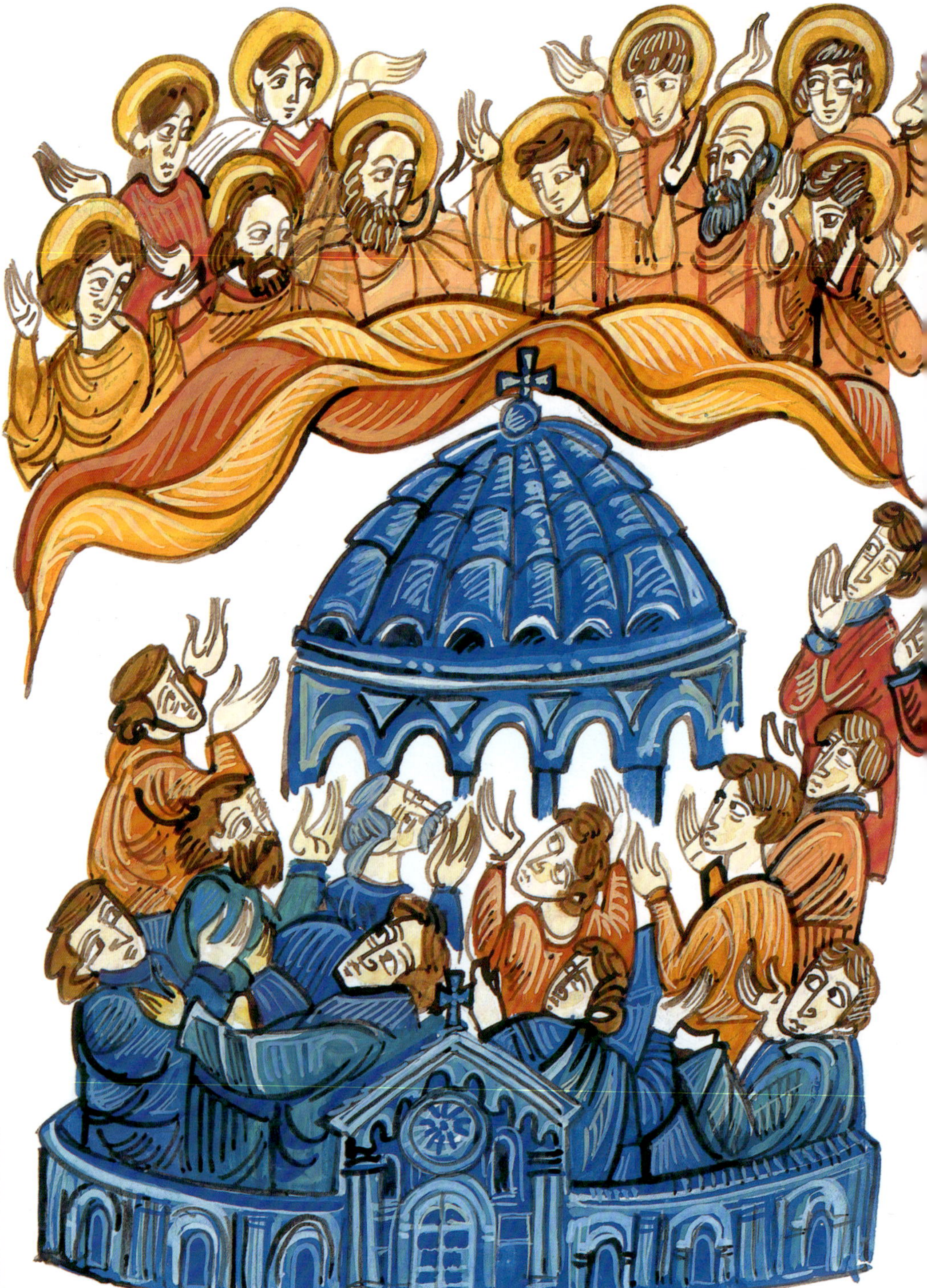

Introduction

If a person does not pray, the Apostles' Creed loses all meaning, it becomes impossible to observe the Commandments, and the Sacraments produce no positive effects. That is why we published this fourth part of the Catechism and dedicated it entirely to prayer, which is the living dialogue with God and the response to his grace.

We begin this section by explaining when and how prayer was born and why humanity is religious. Then we recall those individuals who, according to Holy Scripture, are the ideals who show us how we should pray. Above all, however, we explain the prayer of Jesus, the great offerer of prayer, who expressly taught us to pray in the Lord's Prayer. Next we go on to discuss the prayers of the Church and the various times and ways in which the disciples of the Lord address God. In the last part of the book we include the simplest and most common prayers of the Church. When one memorizes these, one has a precious treasure for one's entire spiritual life.

The illustrations that accompany the text help clarify the discussion. Still, it is intended that children read this section under the guidance of parents or catechists, who can explain and add to the material presented here. But adults can help children grasp the message of this book most effectively by praying with them. This will initiate them into the regular practice and pleasure of prayer. Then prayer will become like bread to them, something that restores and nurtures them daily.

Humanity in Search of God

All of us feel the call of God within us, even if it is in a vague and confused way. All of us read God's message in our own hearts and in the universe that surrounds us, and it is like listening to God's story.

It was God himself who created human beings from nothing, and who imprinted in us the tendency to seek God, the need to pray to him, and a constant uneasiness until we are with him. " For 'in him we live and move and have our being' " (Acts 17:28).

It is our nature, then, to be religious, and God is not far from us. However, sin makes our journey toward God difficult, and along the way we often make serious mistakes. But God has made us so that we might seek him, "even perhaps grope for him" ' (Acts 17:27).

Our religious nature explains so many things about human culture: the origin of religions, the building of holy places, the setting aside of temples dedicated to prayer, the offering of sacrifices, the variety of rituals, the books about and formulas for prayer. However, our sinfulness explains why, instead of adoring the one true God, we have created so many idols and worshipped them instead of the Father.

The Covenant between God and Humanity

Before we could seek God, it was God who sought us. From the very beginning, when God created us from nothing, in his own image and likeness, he gave us the gift of his grace, of his friendship. God did this because of Jesus, his Son, who became a human being.

God revealed himself to human beings by speaking to us in the depths of our hearts and through his creation, which is the work of God's hands and the proclamation of his glory. Our proper response should have been adoration, praise, and thanksgiving. However, instead of praying in joy and appreciation for the gift that we received, we proudly withdrew into ourselves. This is the sin of humanity, yet God has not abandoned us. With the promise of the Savior Jesus, God in his mercy began a history of offering humanity a covenant and forgiveness of our sins. The history of our relationship with him is also the history of prayer.

The Acceptable Gifts of Abel and Noah

Prayer is born in us when we become aware that God has created us from nothing. The first feeling that pervades us is, therefore, adoration, in which we recognize God as the Eternal One, the Infinite One, the Almighty, the Holy One. Yet, though God is high and holy, he has always been close to us, his creatures: he calls us to life and gives us everything because of his love for us.

Prayer is thus a response of gratitude and thanksgiving. This gratitude wells up from the depths of our hearts, the source of prayer, and we express it here before we express it in words or actions. But we also feel the need to show our adoration and gratitude through deeds. Thus, Abel offered the first-born of his flock to God, who appreciated that sacrifice as an expression of Abel's innocent soul. In the same way, Noah and other righteous people like him would sincerely honor God. But God did not appreciate offerings from those with impure motives. God did not accept the offering made by Cain, for example because he could see that Cain did not have a pure heart.

The Prayers of Abraham and Moses

Abraham, the friend of God, stands out as one of the people in the Bible most dedicated to prayer. Abraham's devout nature can be seen in how attentively he listened to the Word of God, in his trusting acceptance of God's promises, and in his steady faith. For Abraham, prayer, which was time spent in the presence of God, was life itself.

Moses was also a great man of prayer. God spoke to him as a friend, "face to face" (Num. 12:8), and in the solitude and silence of Mount Sinai, where he received the Ten Commandments, Moses spent a long time with the Lord, begging him to forgive the people who had chosen to adore the golden calf rather than the true God.

The Prayers of Elijah, Job, Jonah, Hannah, and David

Sacred history is a history of prayer by the faithful, who through their faith welcome the divine gifts of the Word and of grace. We recall the ardent prayer of love and devotion that Elijah, the solitary prophet, prayed to God on the mountain. In response, the Lord came close to Elijah and spoke to him.

Job was also a man of prayer. The Lord put Job's faith to a long and severe test by taking everything away from him. But, although he had some very painful experiences, Job maintained his faith in the mysterious and wise actions of God.

When the prophet Jonah was on a storm-tossed boat, he was thrown overboard and swallowed by a large fish. He prayed for the Lord's help, and God freed him from the fish's stomach. In the same way, the tearful and humble pleas of Hannah were answered when God granted her the gift of a son, Samuel.

Above all, however, it was the prayer of the Psalms that rose up to God throughout the centuries of salvation history. It is thought that most of the Psalms were written by King David, but their song is heard at every liturgy of the Church even today. Over time they came to form the greatest prayer book of all: the Psalter, or Book of Psalms. In the Psalter, God has given us prayers for every situation.

114

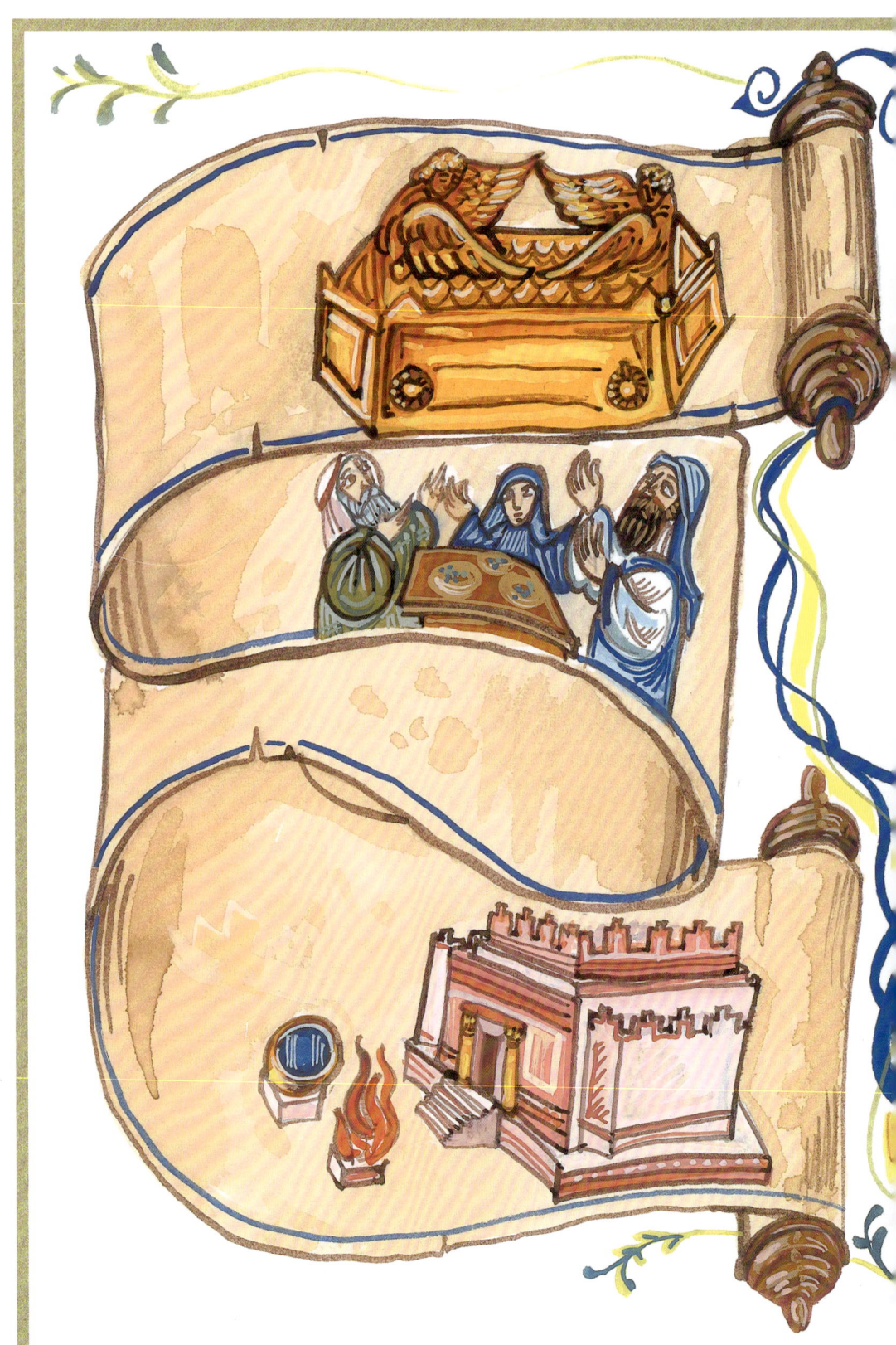

Signs, Places, and Times of Prayer

Since God is spirit, and prayer must originate in our hearts, we can encounter God anywhere and at any time. However, he also speaks and communicates himself to us through signs, which make us aware of his presence. For the Israelites, a special sign of divine presence was the Ark of the Covenant, which they carried with them during their many wanderings.

The Israelites, who were a people of prayer, offered their prayers in a variety of places. When they were not able to worship in the Temple, they gathered in the synagogue on the Sabbath and on Feast Days to read the Word of God, to profess their faith, and to pray. The Israelites also prayed regularly at home — in the morning, at noon, and at night.

The most special place of prayer was the Temple of Jerusalem, where sacrifices were offered and where the great Feast Day were solemnly celebrated to commemorate the miraculous interventions of God throughout history, beginning with Passover.

Three Wonderful Prayers: "Magnificat", "Benedictus", and "Nunc dimittis"

The righteous had waited, praying for the coming of Jesus, the Messiah and Savior, and when he came, prayer became more alive and intense. Scripture has given us three prayers born from the experience of being close to Jesus. After the Lord's Prayer, these are the most beautiful prayers in the entire Bible, and the Church repeats them every day with deep emotion.

The first of these prayers is the "Magnificat", which burst forth from the humble heart of Mary, the Mother of Jesus. God chose her so that he could do "great things" through her, and the Magnificat is her prayer of gratitude to him.

The second prayer is the "Benedictus". It was offered up by Zacharias, the father of John the Baptist, in praise of God's merciful goodness.

The third prayer, the "Nunc dimittis," sprang forth from the relieved soul of the elderly Simeon. The Holy Spirit had told Simeon that he would not die until he had seen the Messiah. When Simeon had taken the baby Jesus in his arms in the Temple, he asked the Lord to let him leave this world in peace.

The Prayer of Jesus

When Jesus came, everything was made new, even prayer. Jesus addressed his prayers to God, his Father, to whom he gave himself with love and devoted joy. Indeed, Jesus spent his life in prayer. He dedicated the quiet and lonely hours of the evening to loving conversation with his Father. And he turned to him during the important moments of his mission on earth and before he performed miracles, giving thanks to the Father and petitioning him with the confidence that his prayers would be heard.

The prayer of Jesus during his agony before his crucifixion is moving and dramatic. Although he begs his Father to save him from the cross, he obediently entrusts himself to his Father's will. He accepts death as an act of love to the Father as well as an act of intercession and supplication for the salvation of all humanity.

"Knock and the door will be opened to you"

Jesus was not the only one who prayed. He also urged his disciples to turn to the Father in his name, confident that God would listen to them as his children. They were to pray with humility, sincerity, patience, and trust. Jesus encouraged them to pray by telling them the parables of the insistent friend who continued to ask for something to eat in the dead of night until he was satisfied, and of the persistent widow who repeatedly asked for justice. Just as these requests were answered, Jesus said, God would answer the disciples' persistent prayers.

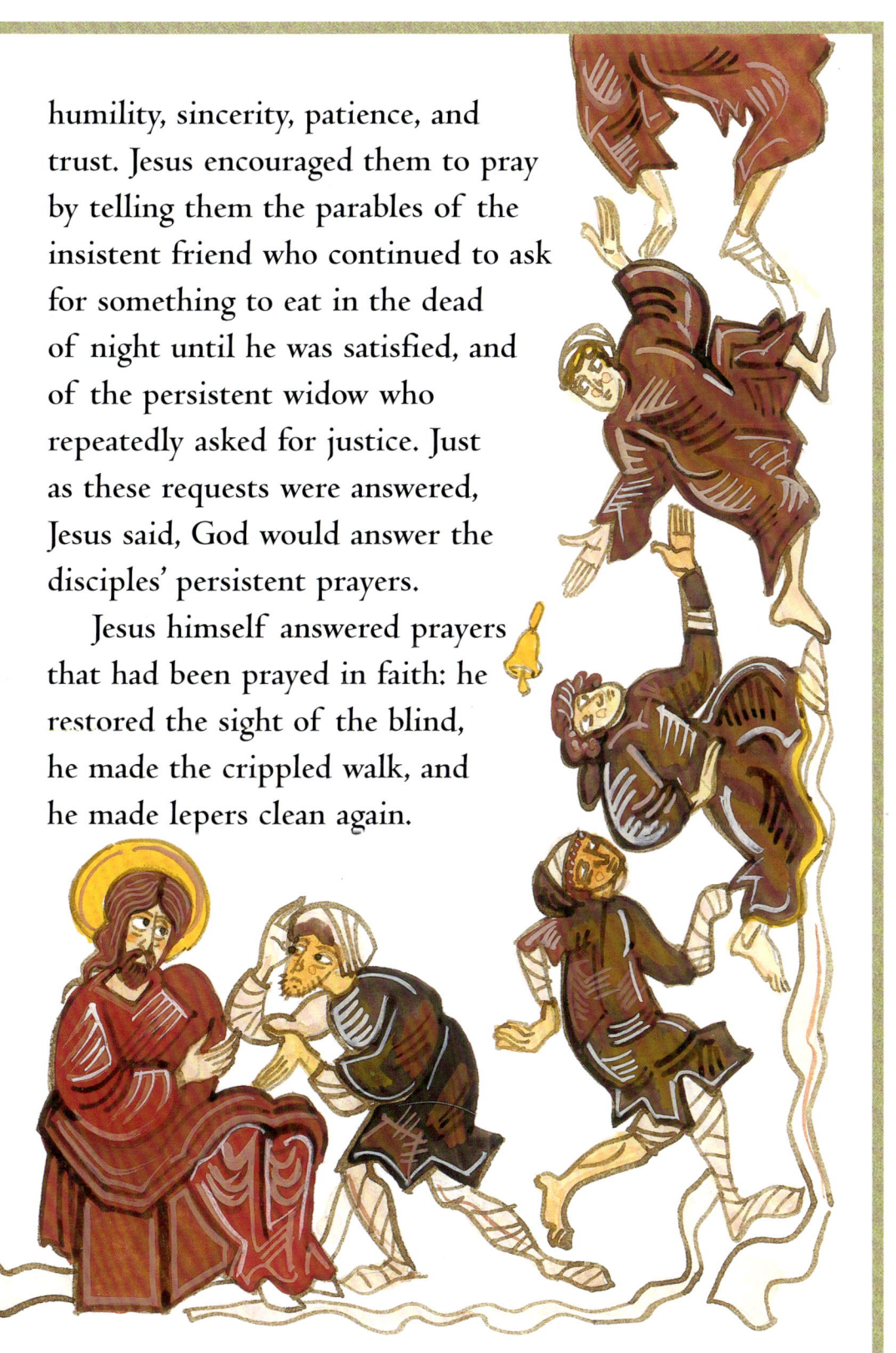

Jesus himself answered prayers that had been prayed in faith: he restored the sight of the blind, he made the crippled walk, and he made lepers clean again.

"Lord, teach us to pray": The Lord's Prayer

The disciples could have learned to pray by listening to Jesus while he prayed. But one day one of them specifically asked him, "Lord, teach us to pray".

Jesus satisfied this request by teaching his disciples the Lord's Prayer. This prayer, which we pray every day, is a summary of all the important elements of the Gospel. However, the Lord did not just leave us words with which to address the Father. Most importantly, he gave us the gift of his Spirit, which filled our hearts with the kind of love that children have for their father. Thus, we too can share in the prayer of Jesus himself, the Son of God.

Saint Paul tells us, " 'God sent the spirit of his Son into our hearts, crying out, 'Abba, Father!' " (Gal. 4:6). It is the Spirit who stirs the desire for prayer in us, and then tells us what to ask in prayer. Even when we pray by ourselves, we never pray alone: we are always in the presence of Jesus and the Holy Spirit.

The Lord's Prayer is the main prayer of the Church, and the prayer prayed most often. It is the model for all other prayers. It is a prayer we should know by heart, so that we can meditate on it deeply and pray it often: it should inspire and shape our entire existence. A true Christian lives the Lord's Prayer.

It will be helpful to examine this prayer more closely and explain it line by line.

*Our Father,
who art
in heaven,
hallowed be
thy name;
thy kingdom
come;*

In communion with Jesus, we address God with the confidence of children who are greatly loved by their Father and who have become one family in him.

With both humility and joy, we invoke God with "Our Father". We also ask that the holiness of God be recognized by all people, and that the Lord Jesus, who is already present among us, will come again in glory and in this way definitively bring to fulfillment the reign of God.

thy will be done on earth as it is in heaven.

The will of God is his mysterious plan of love in action in the world. In the third petition of the Lord's Prayer, we ask that this plan be fulfilled and that we accept it with faith, willingly submitting to it in every circumstance of our lives: in daily work, in health and in sickness, in the various and difficult trials that the Lord may allow in our lives.

In this petition we also ask for insight into God's plan for us, as well as strength to accept this plan. Jesus is always the model of how to do what God wills: in every moment, he is busy doing what is pleasing to the Father.

Give us this day our daily bread; and forgive us our trespasses,

as we forgive those who trespass against us;

Because we are God's children, and he is the Father who provides for us, we ask him with trust for the bread that we need each day to survive. We ask for it for ourselves and for those who are dear to us, with whom we are called to share it. This bread represents everything that we need.

We also need to have God forgive our sins, but in order to receive divine pardon, we must be willing to always forgive others.

and lead us not
into temptation,
but deliver us
from evil.
Amen.

Because of our weakness, it is easy for us to give in to temptation. Recognizing this, we beseech the Father to keep us from yielding to temptation, and to make us participants in the victory of Jesus over the Tempter. We must always be on guard, because the Evil One will always be seeking to ensnare us. He is not just an imaginary figure or a symbol of evil. Jesus called him "a murderer from the beginning", "a liar and the father of lies", and "the prince of this world". Jesus threw him out of heaven, but he can still tempt us to sin. We therefore ask Jesus to deliver us from him.

The Lord's Prayer ends with "Amen", which means "So be it". That single word summarizes all of the desire we have expressed to God and all of our trust in him.

132

The Church at Prayer

The followers of Jesus are faithful to the teaching and commands of their Teacher. They often gather to pray; indeed, the Church is a praying community. If the Church did not pray, it would lose its identity and would no longer be the Church of Christ.

The most solemn and important form of prayer is the liturgy. Here the faithful gather together with the priest to commemorate the works of the Lord, beginning with his passion, death, and resurrection, which are the principal mysteries of our salvation.

For this reason, the most important prayer of the Church is the celebration of the Eucharist, in which we commemorate the Easter mystery and the body and blood of Jesus are really present.

Other important occasions for prayer are the celebration of the other sacraments, and the Liturgy of the Hours, in which the various times of the day are made holy, particularly by praying specially chosen Psalms.

Jesus himself is always present in liturgical prayer, uniting his Church to the prayer that he unceasingly raises to the Father.

Sunday Prayer and Daily Prayer

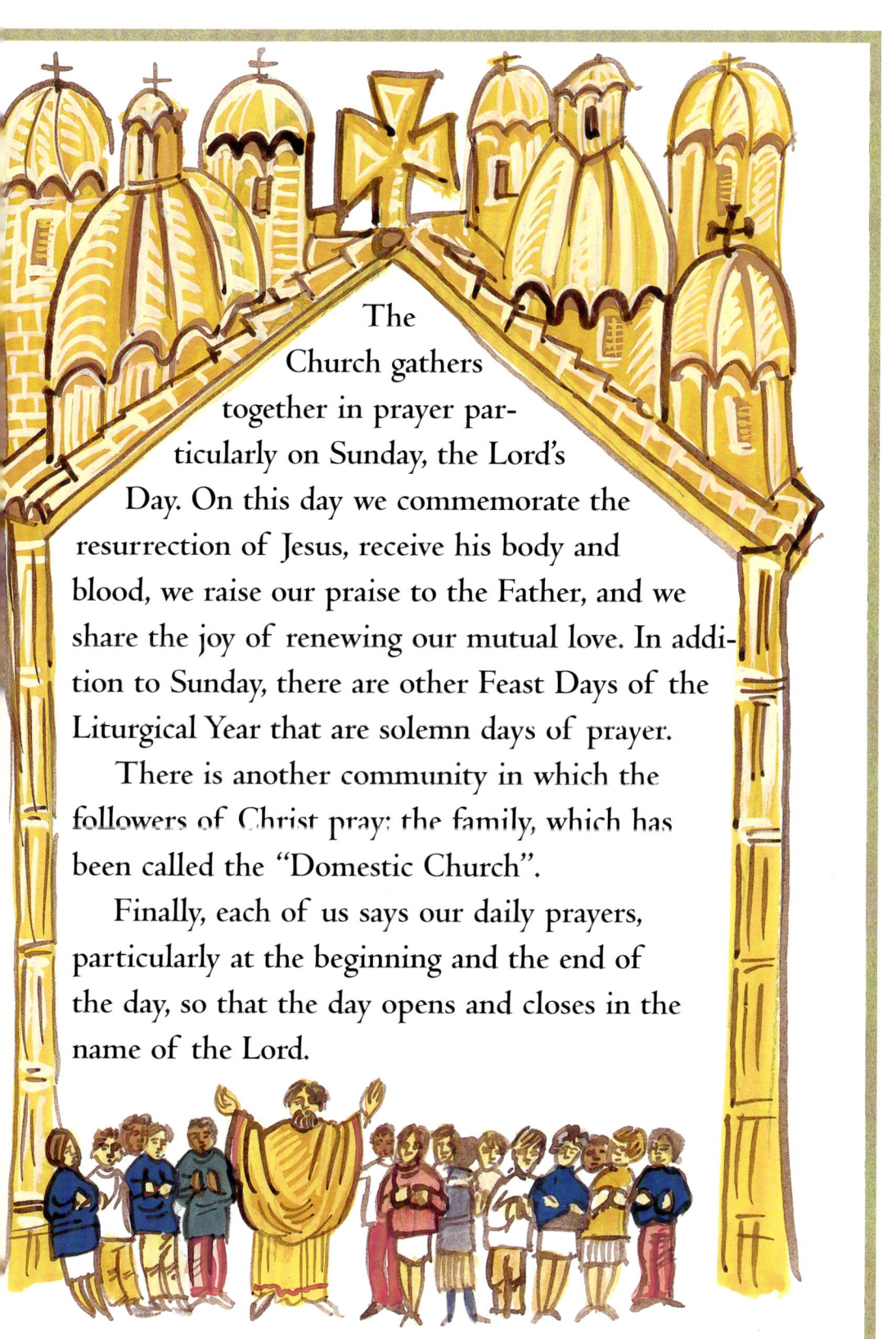

The Church gathers together in prayer particularly on Sunday, the Lord's Day. On this day we commemorate the resurrection of Jesus, receive his body and blood, we raise our praise to the Father, and we share the joy of renewing our mutual love. In addition to Sunday, there are other Feast Days of the Liturgical Year that are solemn days of prayer.

There is another community in which the followers of Christ pray: the family, which has been called the "Domestic Church".

Finally, each of us says our daily prayers, particularly at the beginning and the end of the day, so that the day opens and closes in the name of the Lord.

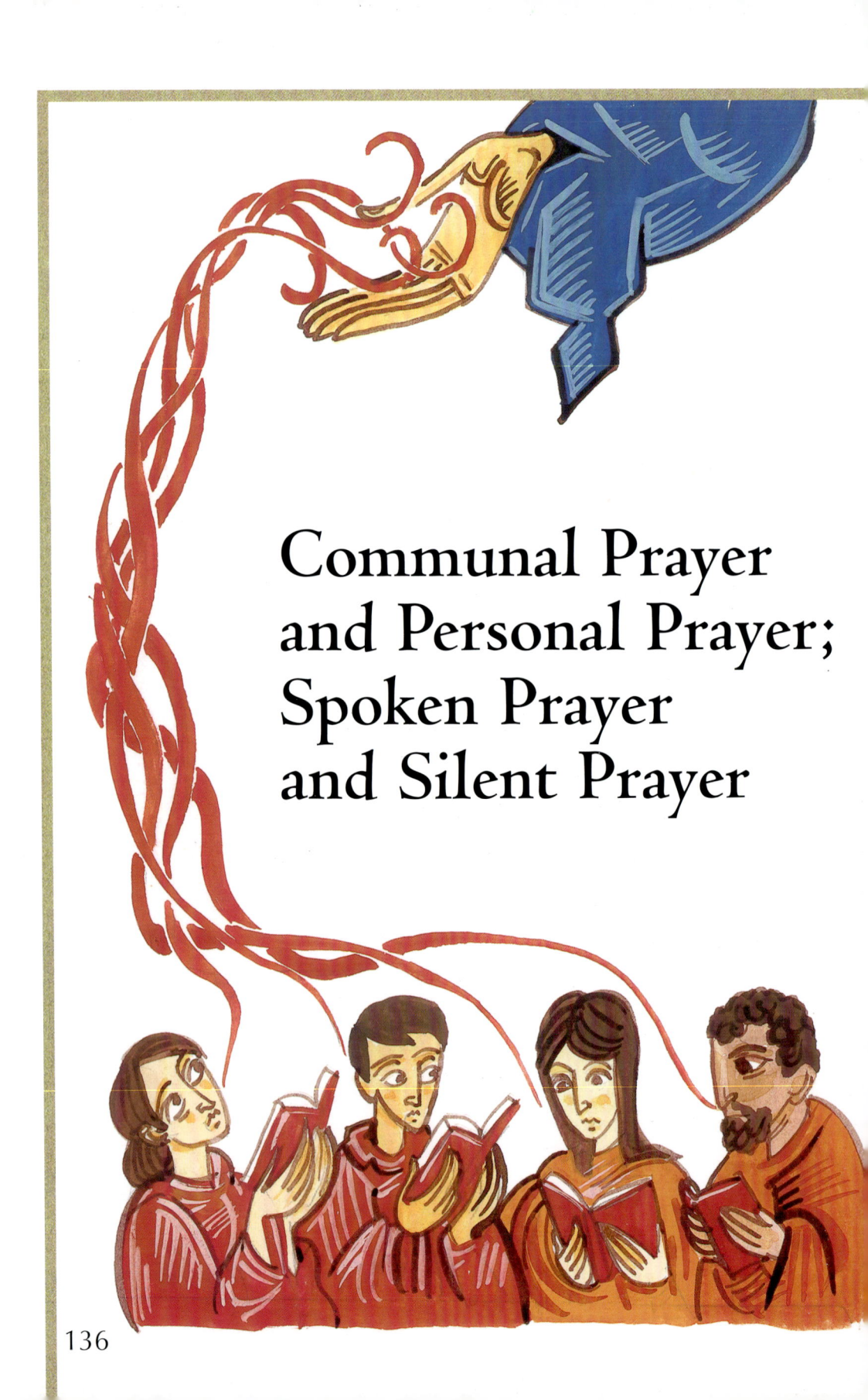

Communal Prayer and Personal Prayer; Spoken Prayer and Silent Prayer

The Lord's followers also pray in contexts other than the liturgy and family prayers. There is prayer with a small group of others, for which Jesus specifically promises his presence. And there is personal prayer, which we offer up in our "inner room", with the door closed, under the gaze of the Father, "who sees in secret" (Matt. 6:5-6). But even private personal prayer is part of the prayer of the entire Church.

Prayer must always come from the heart. We can raise our voices in spoken prayer. But it is also possible to pray silently, by directing our minds to God and allowing our souls to adore him.

Prayers

In addition to the Lord's Prayer, there are other prayers that are cherished and prayed often in the Church — prayers that are brief, simple, and to the point.

Some prayers are directed to the Holy Trinity, others to the Virgin Mary. There is a prayer to our Guardian Angel, and a prayer for the dead. There are morning and evening prayers, and prayers to be said before meals.

It is a good idea to memorize these prayers, so that we can easily and frequently pray them, either by speaking them aloud or, even better, by meditating on them in our hearts.

The Sign of the Cross
In the name of the Father and of the Son and of the Holy Spirit.
Amen.

Glory Be to the Father

Glory be to the Father,
and to the Son,
and to the Holy Spirit.
As it was in the beginning,
is now, and ever shall be,
world without end.
Amen.

The Hail Mary

Hail Mary, full of grace,
the Lord is with thee.
Blessed art thou among women,
and blessed is the fruit
of thy womb, Jesus.
Holy Mary, Mother of God,
pray for us sinners, now,
and at the hour of our death.
Amen.

Angel of God

Angel of God,
my guardian dear,
to whom God's love
commits me here.
Ever this day be at my side,
to light and guard,
to rule and guide.
Amen.

Eternal Rest

Eternal rest,
grant unto them, O Lord.
And let perpetual light
shine upon them.
May they rest in peace.
Amen.

Morning Prayer

I adore you, My God,
and I love you with all my heart.
I thank you for having created me,
for having made me a Christian,
and for having protected me
during the night. I offer you what
I do this day: may all my actions be
in accordance with your divine will, and for your greater
glory. Protect me from sin and from all evil. May your
grace always be with me and those dear to me. Amen.

Blessing of Food

Bless us, O Lord,
and these your gifts,
which we are about to receive
from your bounty.
Through Christ our Lord.
Amen.

Evening Prayer

I adore you, my God,
and I love you with all my heart.
I thank you for having created me,
for having made me a Christian,
and for having protected me
during this day. Forgive me the sins
that I have committed today, and if I have done some good, accept it. Protect me during my sleep, and free me from all danger. May your grace always be with me and with those dear to me. Amen.

Hail, Holy Queen

Hail, holy Queen, Mother of Mercy. Hail, our life, our sweetness, and our hope. To thee do we cry, poor banished children of Eve; to thee do we send up our sighs, mourning and weeping, in this valley of tears. Turn then, most gracious advocate, thine eyes of mercy toward us; and after this our exile, show unto us the blessed fruit of thy womb, Jesus. O clement, O loving, O sweet Virgin Mary.

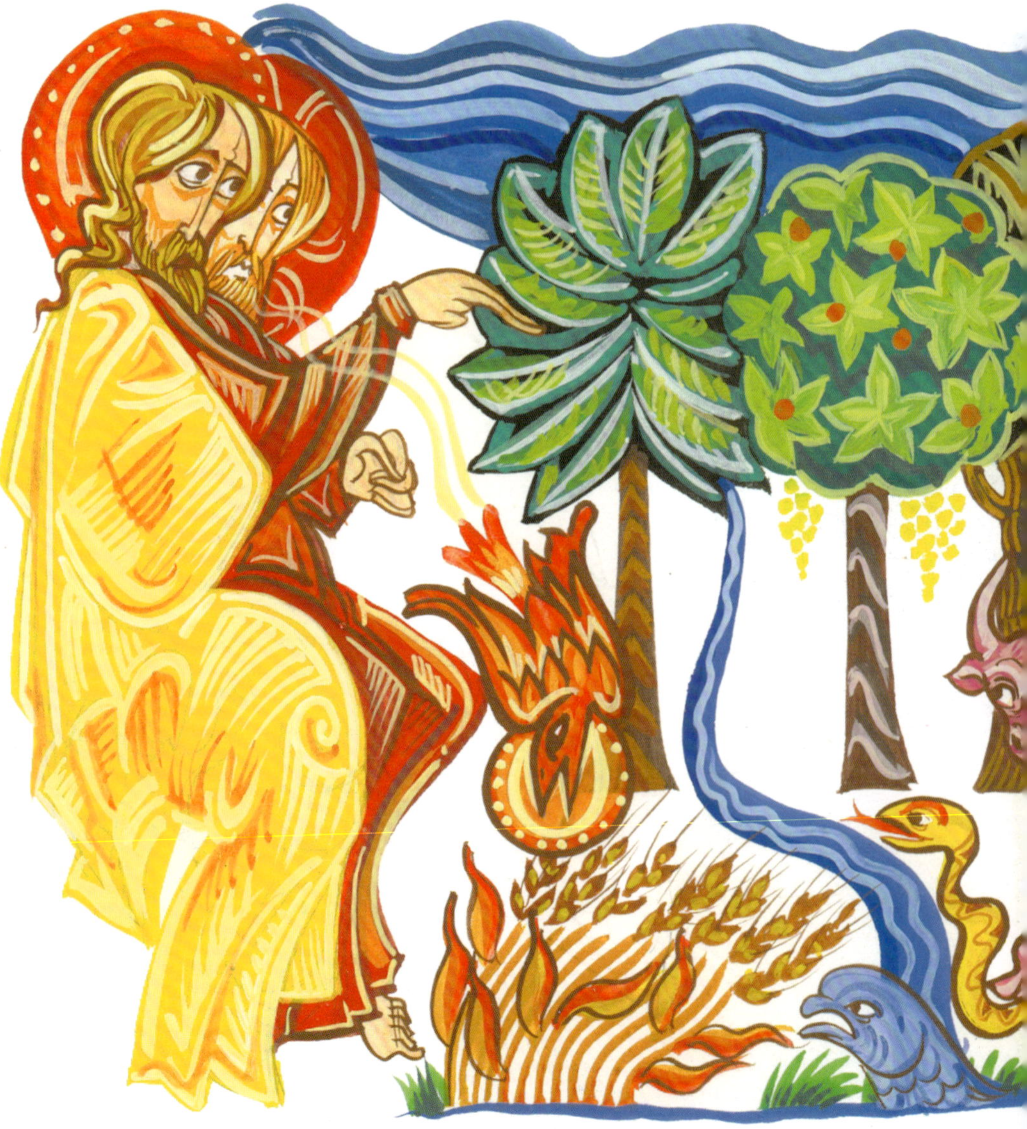

INOS BIFFI is Professor of
Mediaeval and Systematic
Theology at the
Theological Univerity
of Northern Italy, Milan.

FRANCO VIGNAZIA lives
in Italy and is an allustrator,
painter, and sculptor.
He also teaches art
in secondary school.

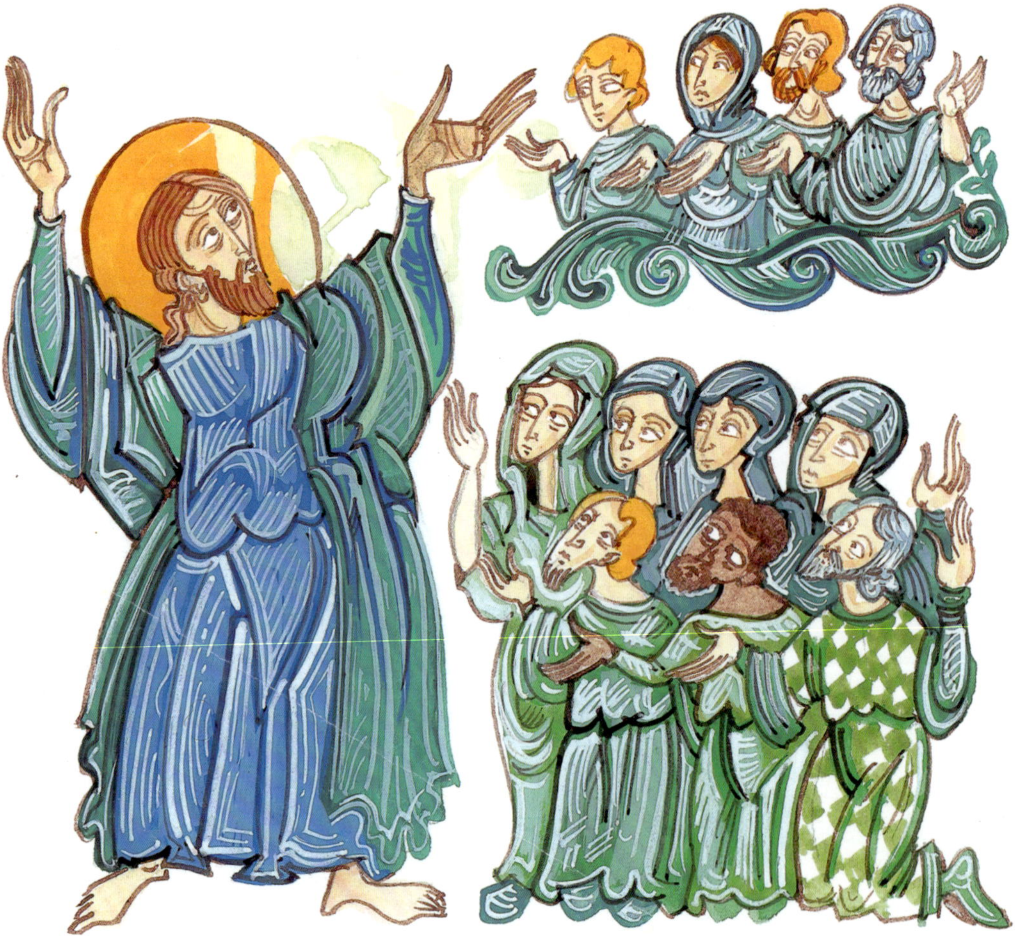